Withdrawn

D0745422

MIGHTY MACHINES
Tow Trucks

by Kay Manolis

BELLWETHER MEDIA • MINNEAPOLIS, MN

Note to Librarians, Teachers, and Parents:

Blastoff! Readers are carefully developed by literacy experts and combine standards-based content with developmentally appropriate text.

Level 1 provides the most support through repetition of high-frequency words, light text, predictable sentence patterns, and strong visual support.

Level 2 offers early readers a bit more challenge through varied simple sentences, increased text load, and less repetition of high-frequency words.

Level 3 advances early-fluent readers toward fluency through increased text and concept load, less reliance on visuals, longer sentences, and more literary language.

Level 4 builds reading stamina by providing more text per page, increased use of punctuation, greater variation in sentence patterns, and increasingly challenging vocabulary.

Level 5 encourages children to move from "learning to read" to "reading to learn" by providing even more text, varied writing styles, and less familiar topics.

Whichever book is right for your reader, Blastoff! Readers are the perfect books to build confidence and encourage a love of reading that will last a lifetime!

This edition first published in 2009 by Bellwether Media.

No part of this publication may be reproduced in whole or in part without written permission of the publisher. For information regarding permission, write to Bellwether Media Inc., Attention: Permissions Department, Post Office Box 19349, Minneapolis, MN 55419.

Library of Congress Cataloging-in-Publication Data
Manolis, Kay.
 Tow trucks / by Kay Manolis.
   p. cm. – (Blastoff! readers. Mighty machines)
 Summary: "Simple text and full color photographs introduce young readers to tow trucks. Intended for students in kindergarten through third grade"–Provided by publisher.
 Includes bibliographical references and index.
 ISBN-13: 978-1-60014-182-9 (hardcover : alk. paper)
 ISBN-10: 1-60014-182-X (hardcover : alk. paper)
 1. Wreckers (Vehicles)–Juvenile literature. 2. Automobiles–Towing–Juvenile literature. I. Title.

TL230.5.W74M36 2009
629.225–dc22   2008012237

Contents

Tow trucks **tow** cars and other vehicles.

A tow truck has a **cab**. The driver sits in the cab.

cab

This tow truck backs up to a car. The car does not work.

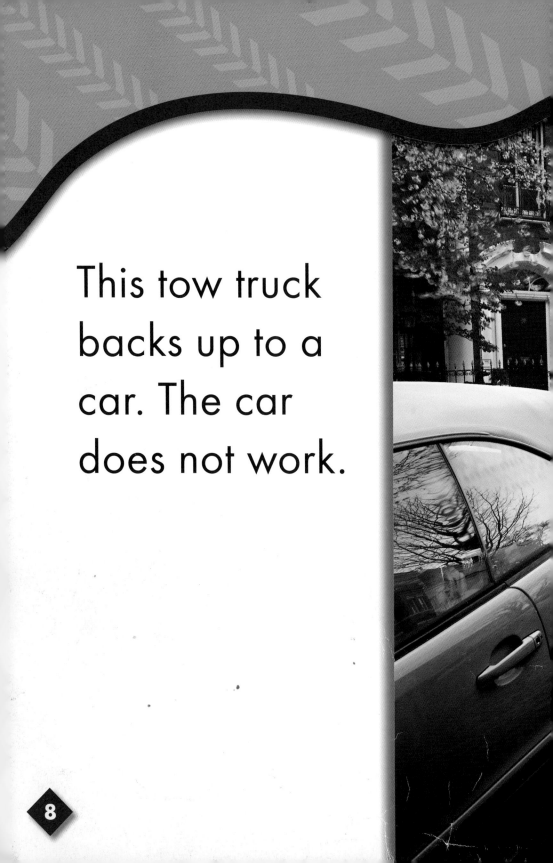

This tow truck has a **wheel lift**. This part grips two tires on the sports car.

wheel lift

The wheel lift raises the two tires off the ground.

This tow truck has a **flatbed**. It carries cars and trucks.

This tow truck lifts a car onto the flatbed.

This tow truck
drives down
the road.

Tow trucks take cars to **repair** shops. Soon the cars will work again.

Glossary

cab—a place where the driver of a vehicle sits

flatbed—a truck bed without walls

repair—to fix

tow—to pull something

wheel lift—a part of a tow truck that grips and lifts two tires of a vehicle

To Learn More

AT THE LIBRARY

DeGezelle, Terri. *Tow Trucks*. Minneapolis, Minn.: Picture Window, 2006.

Steele, Michael Anthony. *I'm a Great Big Tow Truck*. New York: Scholastic, 2003.

Winget, Mary and W. Bryan. *Tow Trucks*. Minneapolis, Minn.: Lerner, 2006.

ON THE WEB

Learning more about mighty machines is as easy as 1, 2, 3.

1. Go to www.factsurfer.com

2. Enter "mighty machines" into search box.

3. Click the "Surf" button and you will see a list of related web sites.

With factsurfer.com, finding more information is just a click away.

Index

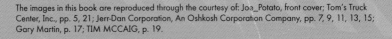

The images in this book are reproduced through the courtesy of: Joe_Potato, front cover; Tom's Truck Center, Inc., pp. 5, 21; Jerr-Dan Corporation, An Oshkosh Corporation Company, pp. 7, 9, 11, 13, 15; Gary Martin, p. 17; TIM MCCAIG, p. 19.